SUPERIOR BANDS IN SIXTEEN V

How to Use This Book

This book may be used in several settings including large and chamber ensembles, and group and private instruction. Following the sixteen-week calendar in *Superior Bands in Sixteen Weeks* will help you to develop greater skills in tone production, intonation, balance (blend), and technique. Your growth as an individual musician benefits you and your ensemble.

Many of the exercises in this book will cover the expanse of your instrument range. Developing players should note that octave choices are available in these exercises. Use the octave that best suits your needs. Add range as you continue to improve.

Ex. B Concert D Harmonic Minor (scale in thirds)

Remember: A good musician always plays with GOOD TONE, GOOD INTONATION, and GOOD TECHNIQUE.

Percussion Rudiments are integrated into the exercises. The director should check to make sure the rudiments are being played correctly. Bells and other treble clef mallet instruments may play the C instrument line.

Good luck!

THE F·J·H MUSIC COMPANY INC.
Frank J. Hackinson

Production: Frank and Gail Hackinson
Production Coordinator: Philip Groeber
Editors: Deborah A. Sheldon, Brian Balmages, Timothy Loest, and Linda Gammon
Cover: Terpstra Design, San Francisco
Text Design and Layout: K. B. Dalzell
Engraving: Tempo Music Press, Inc.
Printer: Tempo Music Press, Inc.

ISBN-13: 978-1-56939-308-6

Table of Contents

Lesson Plan 3

Band Balance 5

SECTION 1: Tone

Band Balance 6

Chromatic Warm-ups 14

Lip Flexibility 18

SECTION 2: Technique

Scales 23

Scales in Thirds 32

Additional Major Scales 41

Arpeggios 45

Breath Control Exercises 54

Chromatic Scales 59

Rhythmic Reinforcement 62

SECTION 3: Balance

Warm-up and Tuning Chorales 65

SECTION 4: Intonation and Percussion Rudiments

Intonation and Tuning 73

Intonation Test 74

Pitch Tendencies and Adjustments 77

Frequently Used Percussion Rudiments 86

SECTION 5: Appendix

Rhythmic Counting 88

Festival Preparation 90

Glossary of Terms 92

Lesson Plan

| | | 1. Tone | | | 2. Technique | | | | | | 3. Balance | 4. Intonation | |
		Band Balance	Chromatic Warm-up	Lip Flexibility	Scales	Scales in Thirds	Arpeggios	Breath Control Exercises	Chromatic Scales	Rhythmic Reinforcement	Warm-up and Tuning Chorales	Intonation Test	Evaluation
Week 1	Page	6	14	18	24	33	46	55	60	62	65	1	
	Exercise	1	1	1	1	1	1	1	1	1	1		
Week 2	Page	6	14	18	24	33	46	55	60	62	65	1	
	Exercise	2	1	2	2	2	2	1	1	2	1		
Week 3	Page	7	14	18	25	34	47	55	60	62	66	2	
	Exercise	3	2	1	3	3	3	1	1	3	2		
Week 4	Page	7	14	18	25	34	47	55	60	62	66	2	
	Exercise	4	2	2	4	4	4	2	1	4	2		
Week 5	Page	8	15	18	26	35	48	55	60	62	67	2	
	Exercise	5	3	1	5	5	5	2	2	5	3		
Week 6	Page	8	15	18	26	35	48	55	60	63	67	3	
	Exercise	6	3	2	6	6	6	2	2	6	3		
Week 7	Page	9	15	18	27	36	49	56	60	63	68	3	
	Exercise	7	4	1	7	7	7	3	2	7	4		
Week 8	Page	9	15	18	27	36	49	56	60	63	68	3	
	Exercise	8	4	2	8	8	8	3	2	8	4		
Week 9	Page	10	15	19	28	37	50	56	61	63	69	4	
	Exercise	9	5	3	9	9	9	3	3	9	5		
Week 10	Page	10	16	19	28	37	50	56	61	63	69	4	
	Exercise	10	5	3	10	10	10	4	3	10	5		
Week 11	Page	11	16	19	29	38	51	56	61	63	70	4	
	Exercise	11	6	4	11	11	11	4	3	11	6		
Week 12	Page	11	16	19	29	38	51	56	61	64	70	5	
	Exercise	12	6	4	12	12	12	4	3	12	6		
Week 13	Page	12	16	20	30	39	52	57	61	64	71	5	
	Exercise	13	7	5	13	13	13	5	4	13	7		
Week 14	Page	12	17	20	30	39	52	57	61	64	71	5	
	Exercise	14	7	5	14	14	14	5	4	14	7		
Week 15	Page	13	17	22	31	40	53	57	61	64	72	6	
	Exercise	15	8	6	15	15	15	5	4	15	8		
Week 16	Page	13	17	22	31	40	53	58	61	64	72	6	
	Exercise	16	8	6	16	16	16	6	4	16	8		

BB204

Two Keys to Becoming a Successful Musician

Proper Playing Position

- Sit on the **edge** of the chair
- Keep feet **flat** on the floor
- **Quietly listen** for instructions

Good Breathing Habits

- **Breathe deeply** and with the diaphragm
- Release the air **slowly with control**

Band Balance

Balance in the ensemble can be attributed to listening, good tone production, accurate intonation, and blend. The Balance Pyramid will help you understand the role of your instrument in the ensemble sound. Study the chart and these suggestions.

- Listen to yourself. Your sound should blend with the full ensemble. If it does not, make adjustments to blend.

- Listen to your section. The section sound should blend with the full ensemble. If it does not, make adjustments to blend.

- After making necessary adjustments, listen again. If you still don't hear a good blend, tone quality may be a concern. Make necessary adjustments (air stream and breath support, posture, embouchure, reed, tuning slide, mouthpiece, barrel).

- After making those adjustments, listen again. If you still don't hear a good blend, intonation may be a concern. Make necessary adjustments (air stream and breath support, posture, embouchure, reed, tuning slide, mouthpiece, barrel).

Use the following chart or Balance Pyramid* to adjust your sound and balance within the band.

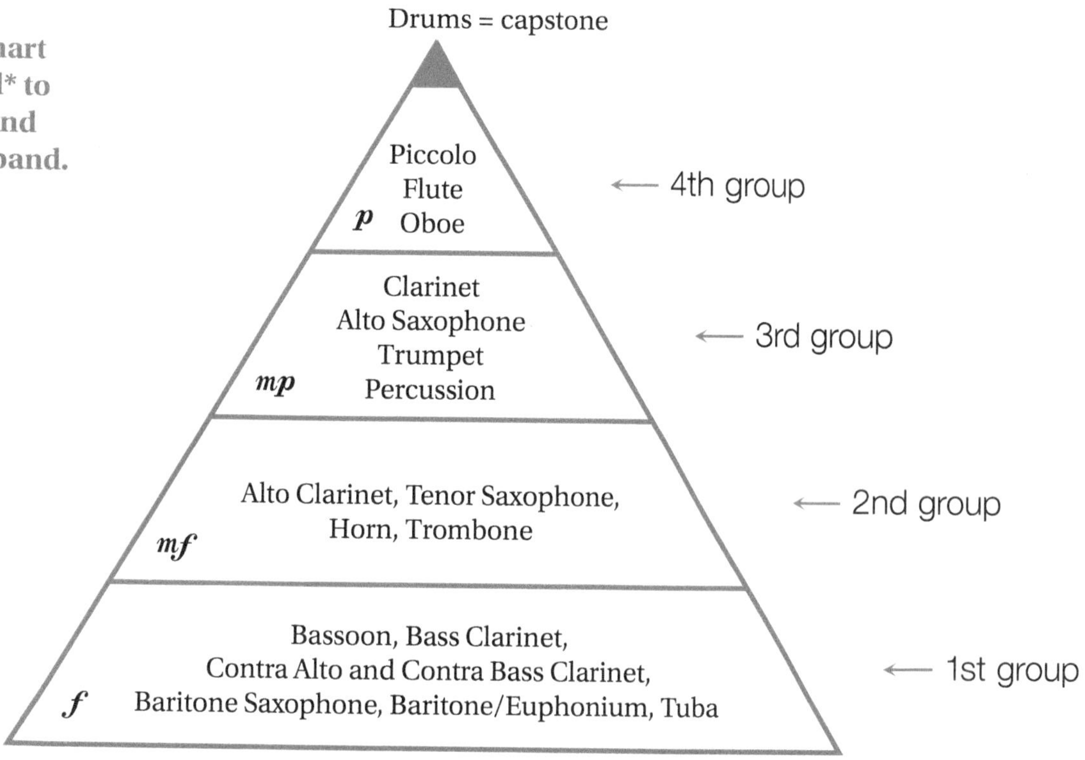

Drums = capstone

Piccolo
Flute
p Oboe ← 4th group

Clarinet
Alto Saxophone
Trumpet
mp Percussion ← 3rd group

Alto Clarinet, Tenor Saxophone,
Horn, Trombone ← 2nd group
mf

Bassoon, Bass Clarinet,
Contra Alto and Contra Bass Clarinet,
Baritone Saxophone, Baritone/Euphonium, Tuba ← 1st group
f

Notes to the Director

1. Start by using a tuning note (concert B♭, concert F).

2. Select other notes to train students through the range of the instrument.

3. Always start by using the first group (refer to pyramid), followed by the second, then the third, and finally the fourth. Conduct so that subsequent groups know to listen and play to blend rather than play louder than the previous group.

4. Use compare and contrast techniques to reinforce the sound of good balance. Allow the group to perform with incorrect balance and instruct them to listen. Discuss the qualities of that sound and follow up with a performance using appropriate blend.

Taken from "Effective Performance of Band Music" by W. Francis McBeth, published by Southern Music.

SECTION 1: Tone

Band Balance

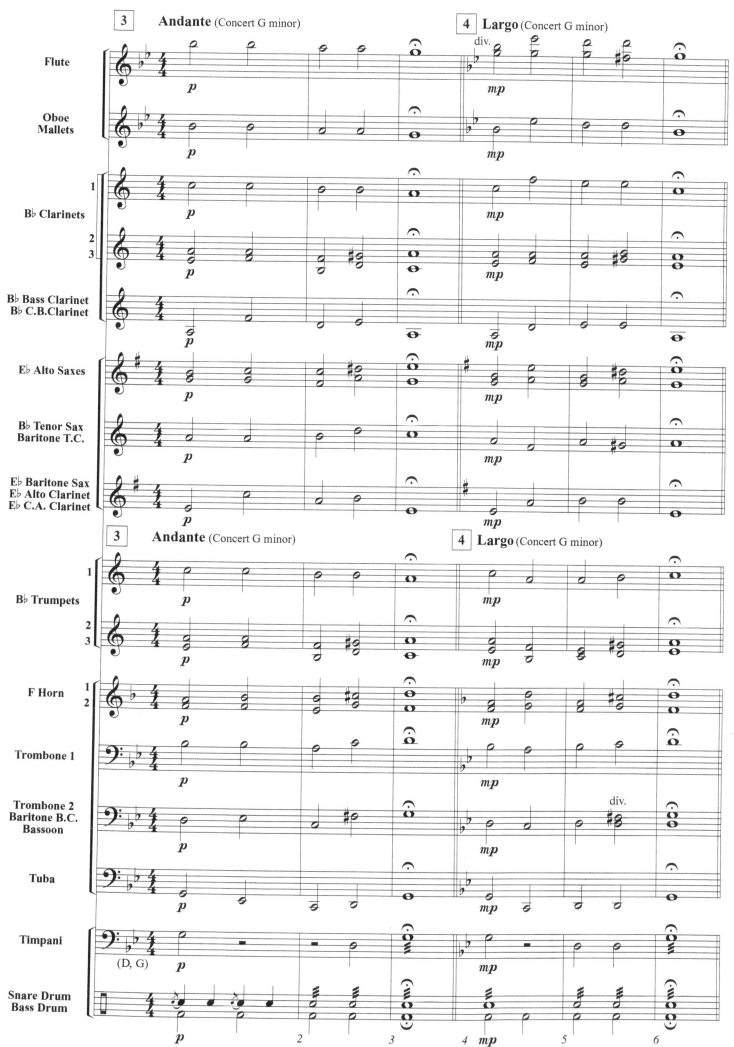

8

BB204

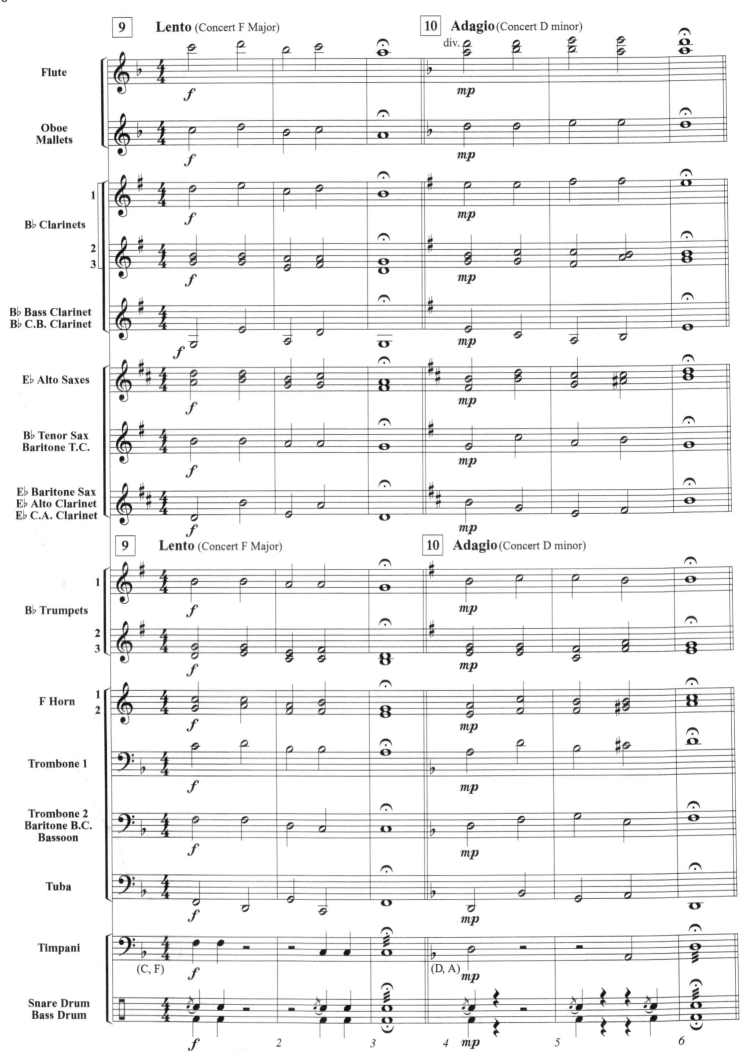

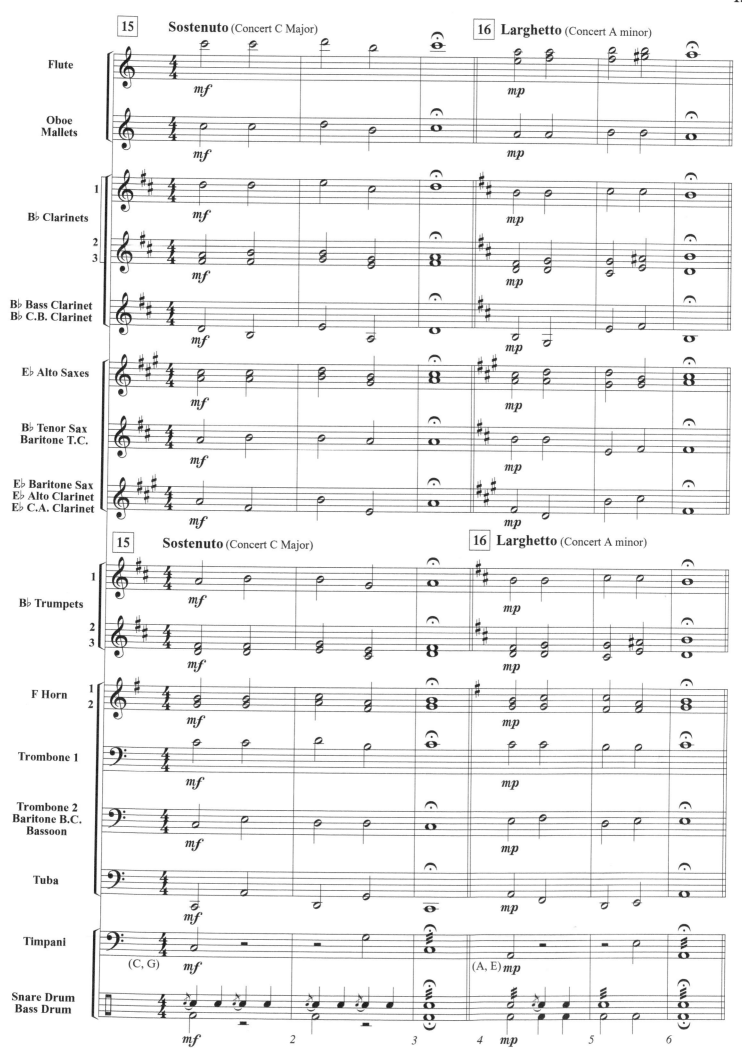

Chromatic Warm-ups

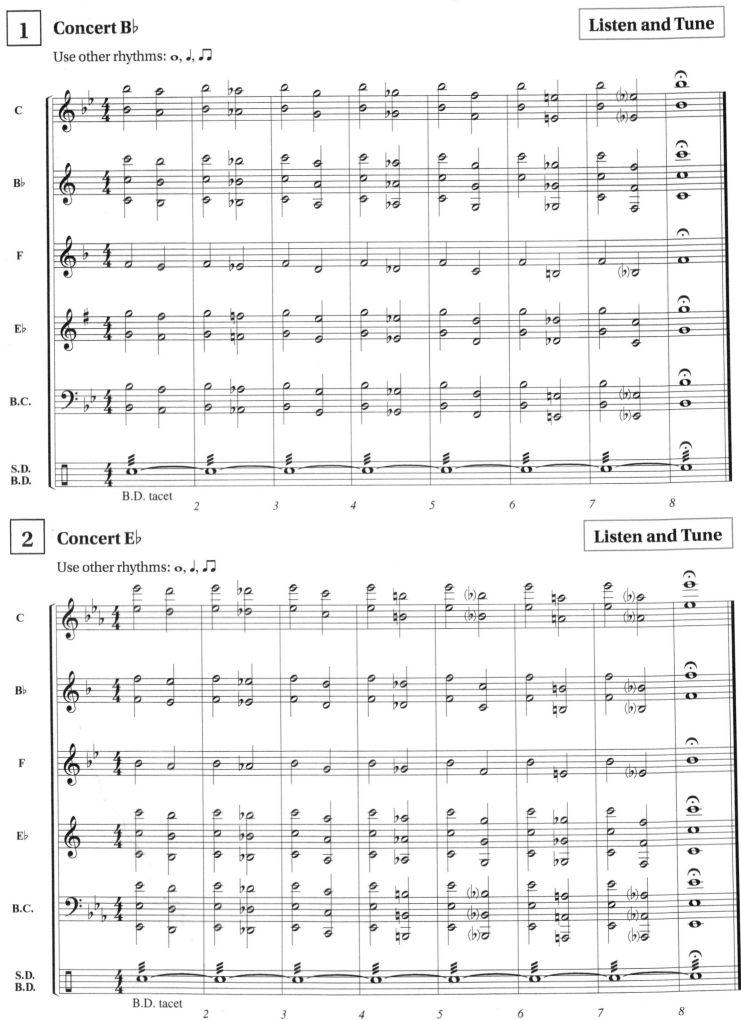

BB204

3 **Concert F**

Listen and Tune

Use other rhythms: 𝅝, 𝅘𝅥, 𝅘𝅥𝅮𝅘𝅥𝅮

4 **Concert A♭**

Listen and Tune

Use other rhythms: 𝅝, 𝅘𝅥, 𝅘𝅥𝅮𝅘𝅥𝅮

BB204

5 **Concert D♭**

Use other rhythms: o, ♩, ♫

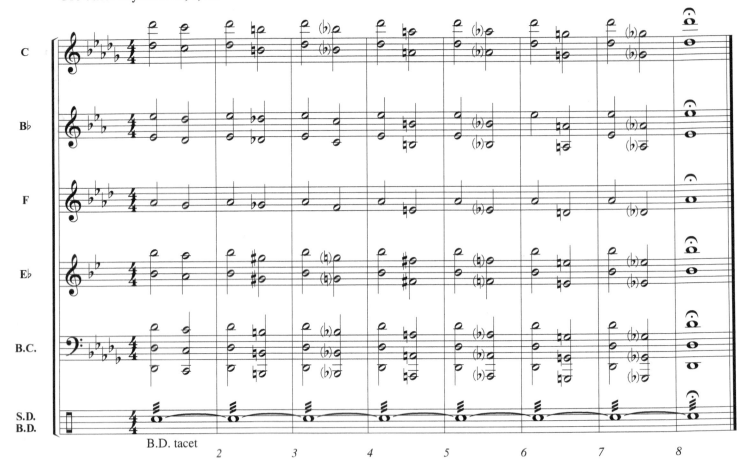

C

B♭

F

E♭

B.C.

S.D.
B.D.

B.D. tacet

2   3   4   5   6   7   8

6 **Concert C**

Listen and Tune

Use other rhythms: o, ♩, ♫

C

B♭

F

E♭

B.C.

S.D.
B.D.

B.D. tacet

2   3   4   5   6   7   8

7 **Concert G**

Listen and Tune

Use other rhythms: o, ♩, ♫

8 **Concert D**

Listen and Tune

Use other rhythms: o, ♩, ♫

Lip Flexibility*
VARY TEMPO

Brass Players Must Do Every Day

*Brass players should use same fingering/position for entire measure (Horn when possible).

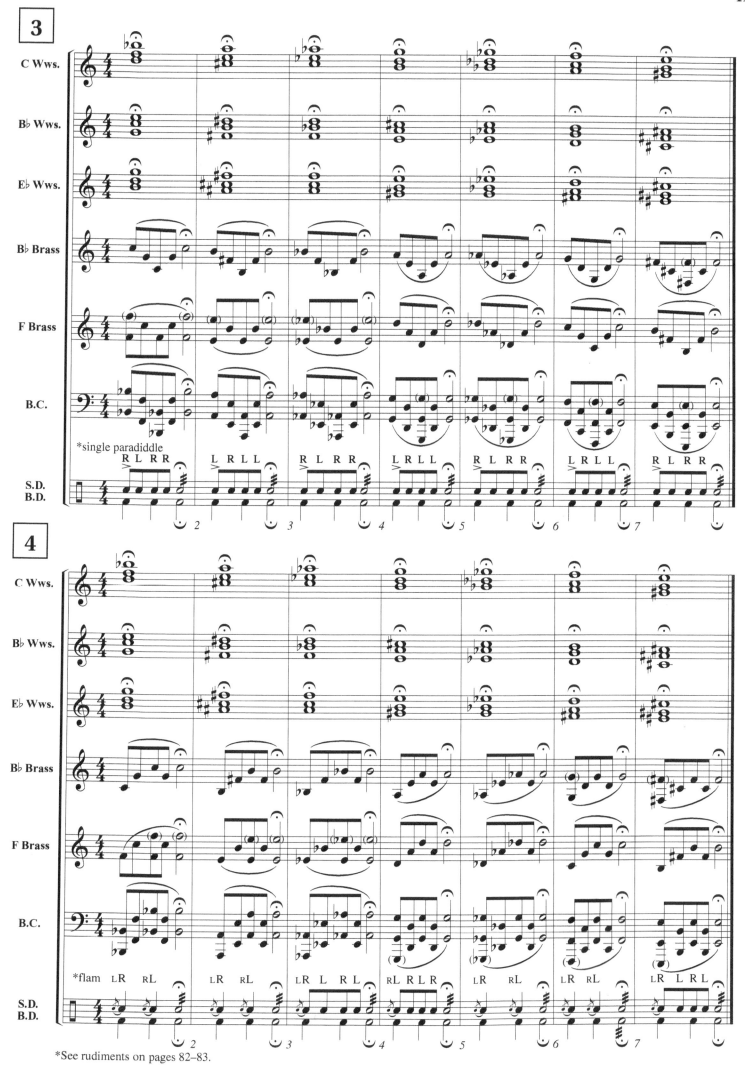

*single paradiddle

*flam

*See rudiments on pages 82–83.

20

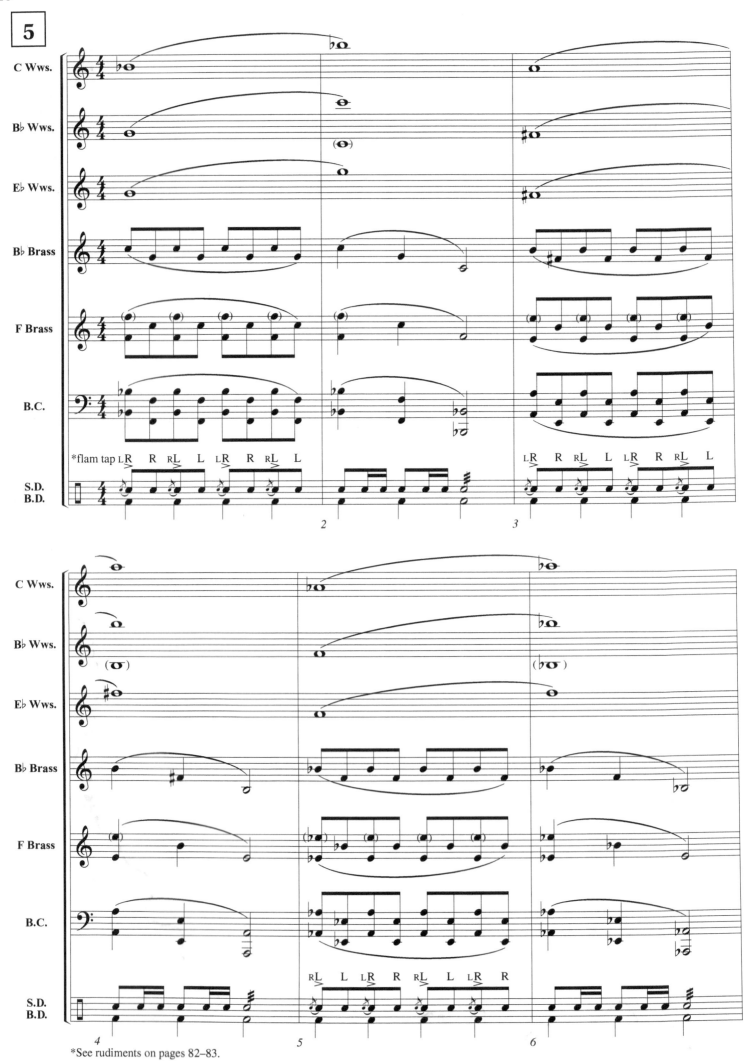

*See rudiments on pages 82–83.

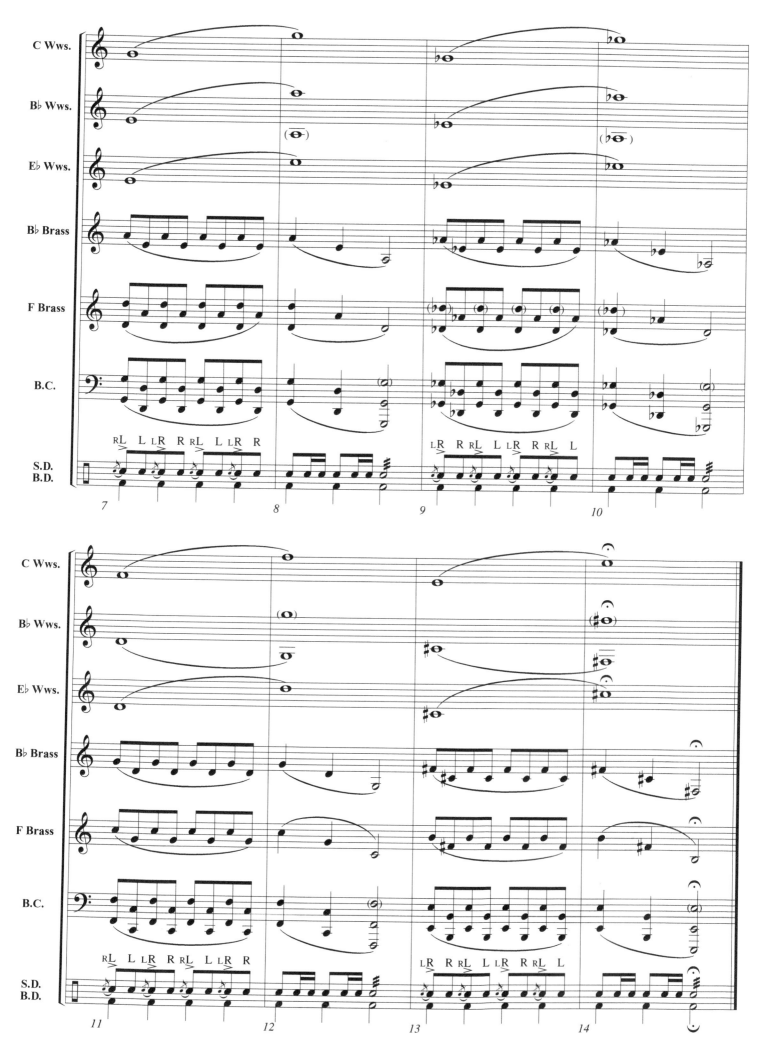

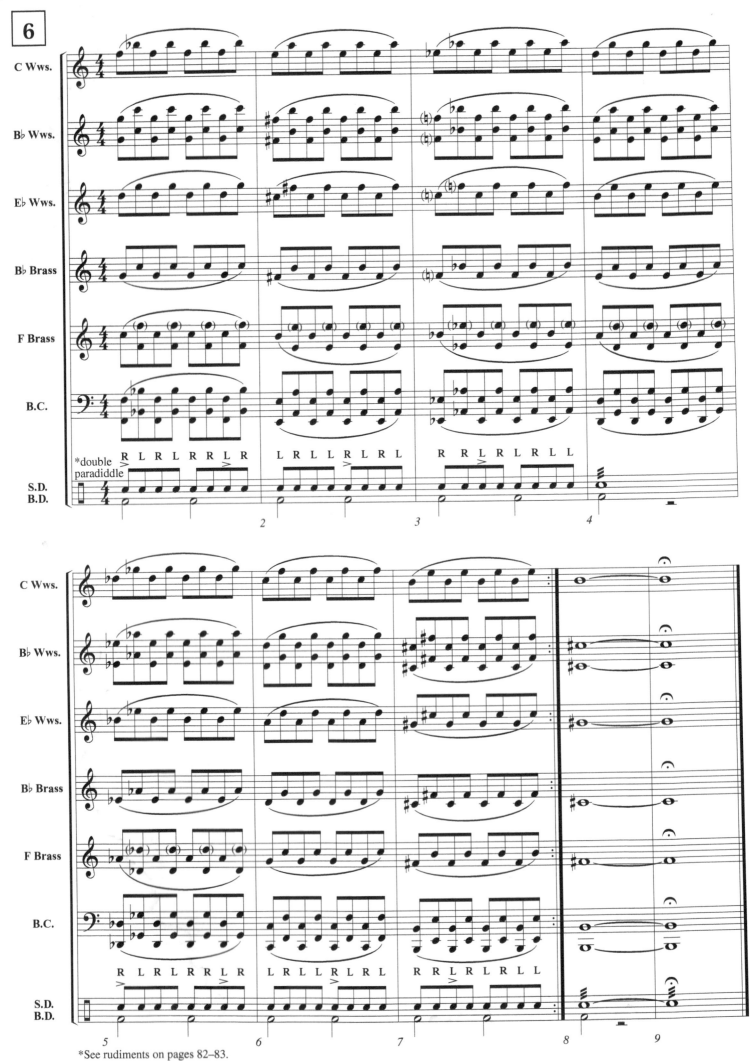

*See rudiments on pages 82–83.

SECTION 2: Technique
Scales

The following patterns may be used for an entire drill or one pattern may be used in the ascending and another in the descending part of the scale. Rehearse these patterns using various tempi. Work to perform *all scale exercises in one breath* and use different dynamic levels.

1 Concert B♭ Major

Work to perform in one breath. Use different dynamic levels and articulations.

2 Concert G Harmonic minor

*See rudiments on pages 82–83.

3 **Concert E♭ Major**

*paradiddle

4 **Concert C Harmonic minor**

*flam tap

*See rudiments on pages 82–83.

26

5 **Concert F Major**

6 **Concert D Harmonic minor**

*flam paradiddle

*See rudiments on pages 82–83.

BB204

7 **Concert A♭ Major**

8 **Concert F Harmonic minor**

BB204

9 **Concert D♭ Major**

10 **Concert B♭ Harmonic minor**

*See rudiments on pages 82–83.

11 **Concert C Major**

*double paradiddle

12 **Concert A Harmonic minor**

*paradiddle

*See rudiments on pages 82–83.

13 **Concert G Major**

14 **Concert E Harmonic minor**

*See rudiments on pages 82–83.

15 **Concert D Major**

C

B♭

F

E♭

B.C.

*flam
paradiddle-diddle

S.D.
B.D.

16 **Concert B Harmonic minor**

C

B♭

F

E♭

B.C.

S.D.
B.D.

*See rudiments on pages 82–83.

Scales in Thirds

The following patterns may be used for an entire drill or one pattern may be used in the ascending and another in the descending part of the scale. Rehearse these patterns using various tempi. Work to perform *all scale exercises in one breath* and use different dynamic levels.

1.

8.

2.

9.

3.

10.

4.

11.

5.

12.

6.

13.

7.

1 ## Concert B♭ Major Scale

Work to perform in one breath. Use different dynamic levels and articulations.

2 ## Concert G Harmonic minor Scale

*See rudiments on pages 82–83.

3 **Concert E♭ Major Scale**

4 **Concert C Harmonic minor Scale**

*See rudiments on pages 82–83.

5 **Concert F Major Scale**

6 **Concert D Harmonic minor Scale**

*flam paradiddle

*See rudiments on pages 82–83.

7 **Concert A♭ Major Scale**

8 **Concert F Harmonic minor Scale**

*See rudiments on pages 82–83.

9 **Concert D♭ Major Scale**

10 **Concert B♭ Harmonic minor Scale**

*See rudiments on pages 82–83.

38

11 Concert C Major Scale

12 Concert A Harmonic minor Scale

*See rudiments on pages 82–83.

13 **Concert G Major Scale**

14 **Concert E Harmonic minor Scale**

*single drag tap

*See rudiments on pages 82–83.

15 Concert D Major Scale

16 Concert B Harmonic minor Scale

*See rudiments on pages 82–83.

Additional Major Scales

17 **Concert A Major Scale**

Work to perform in one breath. Use different dynamic levels and articulations.

18 **Concert E Major Scale**

*The director may explain the enharmonic spelling of this key.

19 **Concert B♭ Major Scale**

20 **Concert G♭ Major Scale**

*The director may explain the enharmonic spelling of this key.

21 Concert F♯ Major Scale

22 Concert C♭ Major Scale

*The director may explain the enharmonic spelling of this key.

23 **Concert C♯ Major Scale**

*The director may explain the enharmonic spelling of this key.

PRACTICE! PRACTICE! PRACTICE!

Arpeggios

The following patterns may be used for an entire drill or one pattern may be used in the ascending and another in the descending part of the scale. Rehearse these patterns using various tempi. Work to perform **all scale exercises in one breath** and use different dynamic levels.

1.

7.

2.

8.

3.

9.

4.

10.

5.

11.

6.

12.

1 Concert B♭ Major Scale

Work to perform in one breath. Use different dynamic levels and articulations.

2 Concert G minor Arpeggio

*See rudiments on pages 82–83.

3 **Concert E♭ Major Arpeggio**

4 **Concert C minor Arpeggio**

5 **Concert F Major Arpeggio**

6 **Concert D minor Arpeggio**

*See rudiments on pages 82–83.

7 | Concert A♭ Major Arpeggio

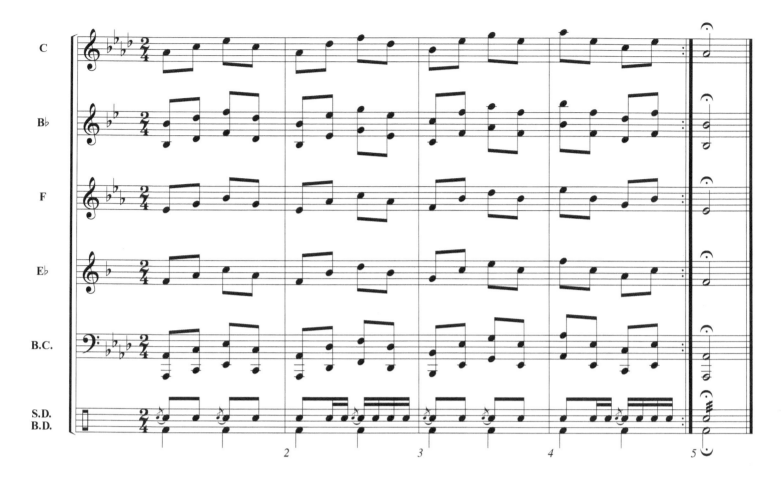

8 | Concert F minor Arpeggio

9 **Concert D♭ Major Arpeggio**

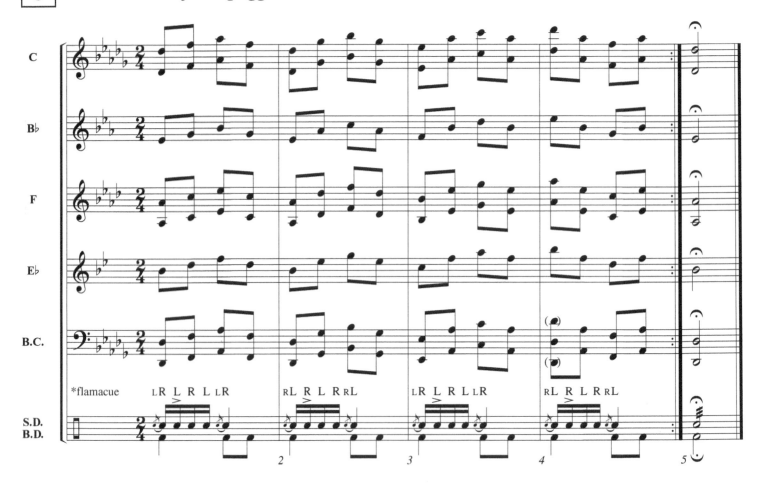

*flamacue

10 **Concert B♭ minor Arpeggio**

*flam tap

*See rudiments on pages 82–83.

11 Concert C Major Arpeggio

12 Concert A minor Arpeggio

*See rudiments on pages 82–83.

13 **Concert G Major Arpeggio**

14 **Concert E minor Arpeggio**

*lesson 25

*See rudiments on pages 82–83.

15 **Concert D Major Arpeggio**

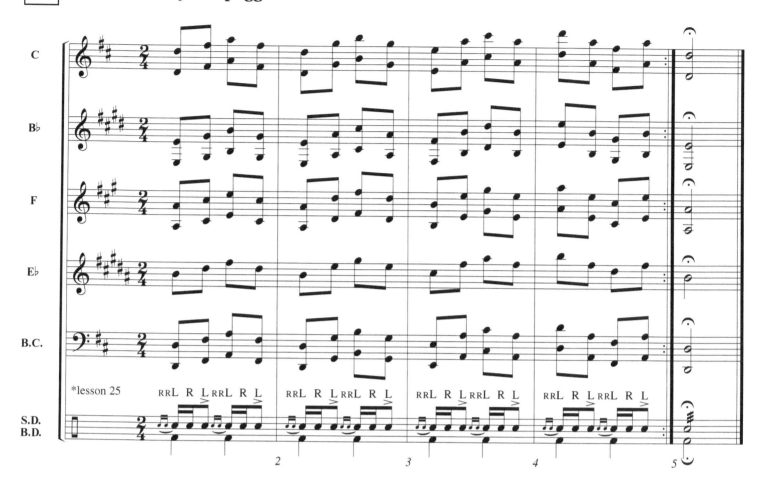

*lesson 25

16 **Concert B minor Arpeggio**

*drag paradiddle #2

*See rudiments on pages 82–83.

Breath Control Exercises

All of these drills must be played in *one breath*.
Try these patterns to reinforce skills in addition to breath control.

1.

2.

3.

4.

5.

6.

7.

8.

9.

10.

11.

12.

1 **Breath Control Exercise**

Play in one breath!

2 **Breath Control Exercise**

*See rudiments on pages 82–83.

3 **Breath Control Exercise**

4 **Breath Control Exercise**

*See rudiments on pages 82–83.

5 **Breath Control Exercise**

*See rudiments on pages 82–83.

58

6 | Breath Control Exercise

*flam tap

*See rudiments on pages 82–83.

BB204

Chromatic Scales

Changing the rhythm of these scales will add variety. The suggested weekly outline is one way to approach chromatic training. Winds and pitched percussion should play the patterns in the first measure. Non-pitched percussion should play the patterns in the second measure. Articulation patterns found in the first scale section of the book may be used with the chromatic scales in a variety of ways to add interest.

1 | Concert B♭ Chromatic Scale

C

B♭

F

E♭

B.C.

Perform rhythm that corresponds to week no. (see page 59)

S.D.
B.D.

2 | Concert E♭ Chromatic Scale

C

B♭

F

E♭

B.C.

Perform rhythm that corresponds to week no. (see page 59)

S.D.
B.D.

3 **Concert F Chromatic Scale**

Perform rhythm that corresponds to week no. (see page 59)

4 **Concert A♭ Chromatic Scale**

Perform rhythm that corresponds to week no. (see page 59)

Rhythmic Reinforcement

1. Work for success in this section by following this method:

      A. Count each exercise aloud.

      B. Clap each exercise.

      C. Breathe, articulate, and finger each exercise with the instrument in playing position.

      D. Play the exercise.

2. Perform each exercise on a given pitch, or allow each student to choose a different pitch that will result in a little dissonance but could be fun and interesting.

PERCUSSION — choose any mallet or non-mallet instrument and play each exercise.

64

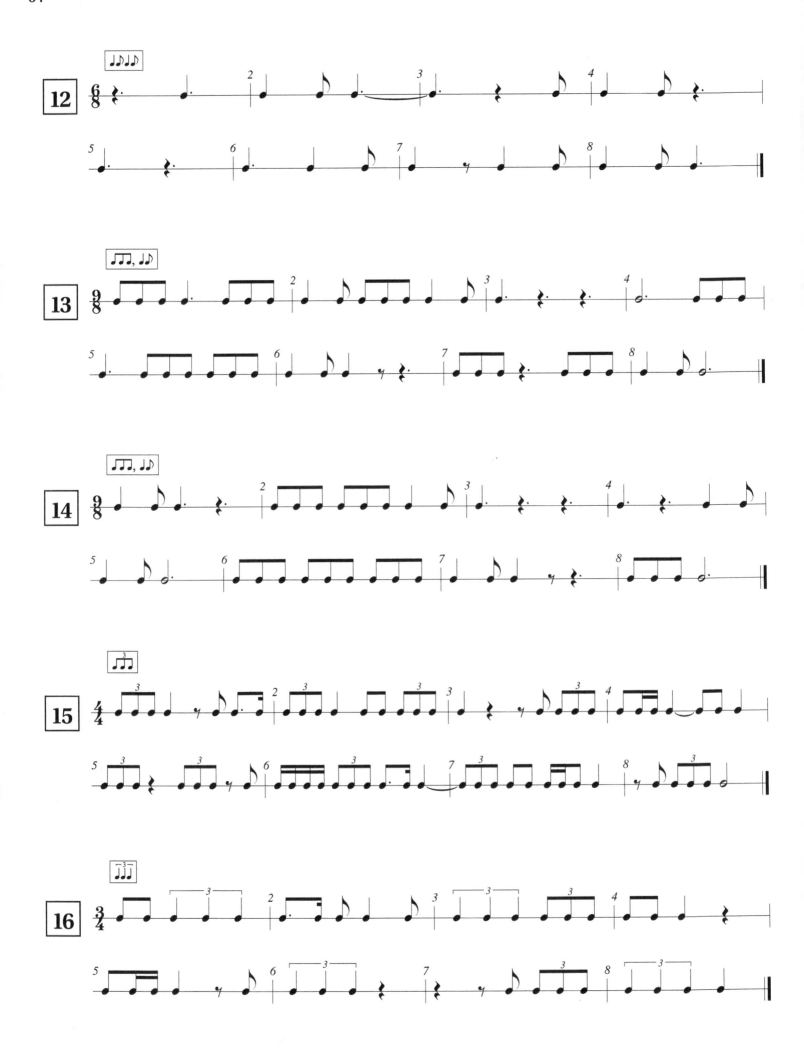

SECTION 3: Balance
Warm-up and Tuning Chorales

1 **Concert B♭ Warm-up and Tuning Chorale**

Vary tempi and dynamic levels.

Listen, Balance, and Tune

66

2 Concert E♭ Warm-up and Tuning Chorale

Vary tempi and dynamic levels.

Listen, Balance, and Tune

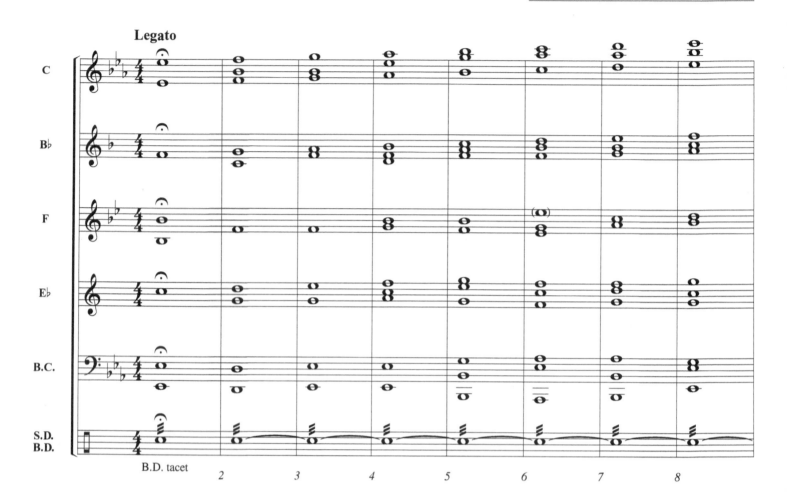

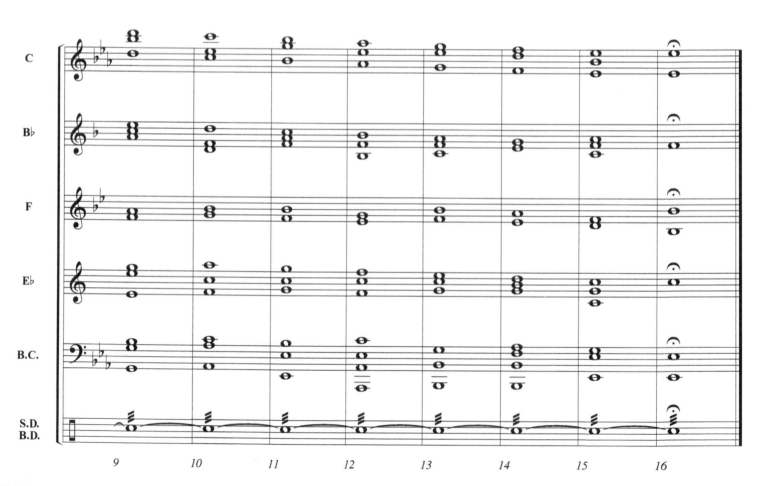

BB204

3 **Concert F Warm-up and Tuning Chorale**

Vary tempi and dynamic levels.

Listen, Balance, and Tune

4 Concert A♭ Warm-up and Tuning Chorale

Vary tempi and dynamic levels.

Listen, Balance, and Tune

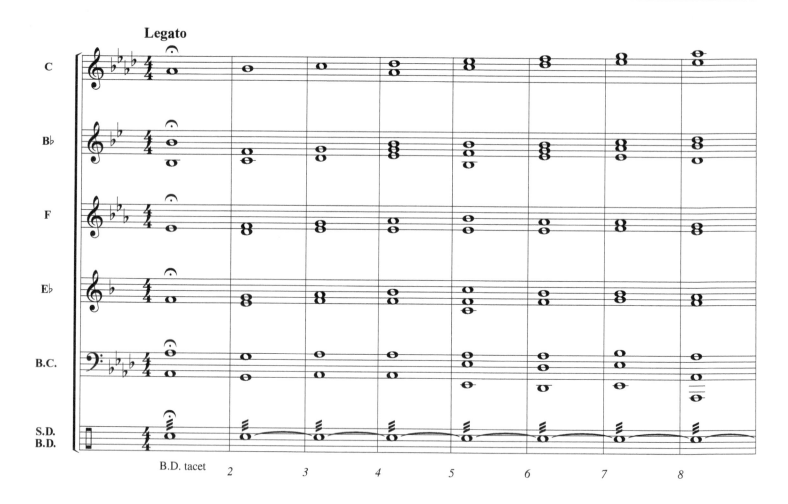

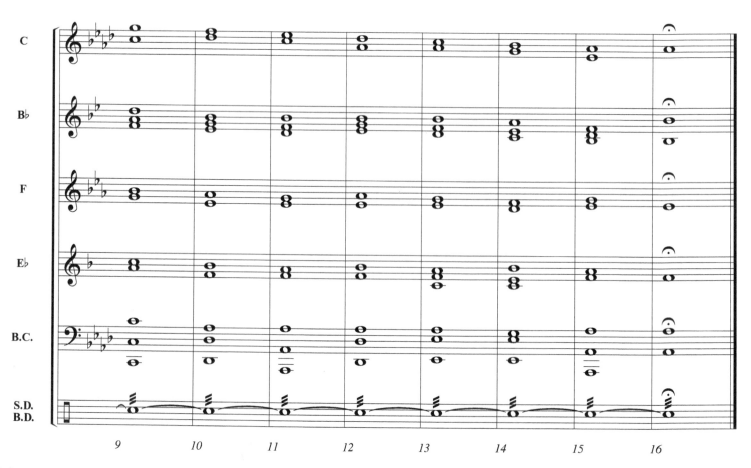

5 **Concert D♭ Warm-up and Tuning Chorale**

Vary tempi and dynamic levels.

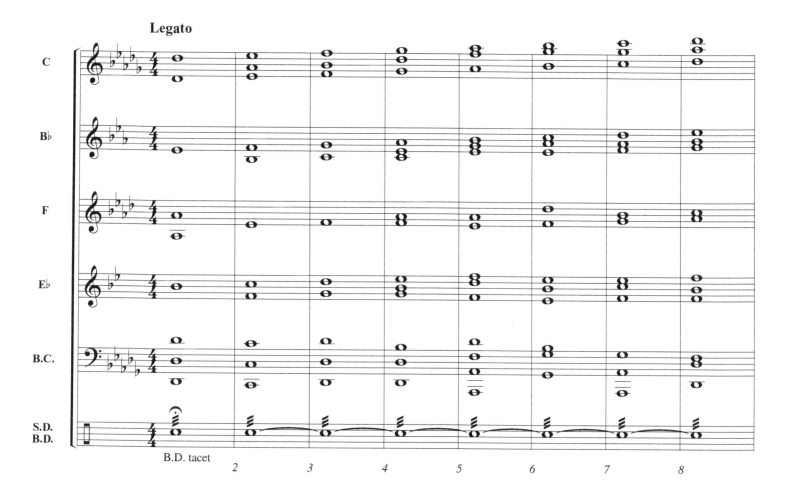

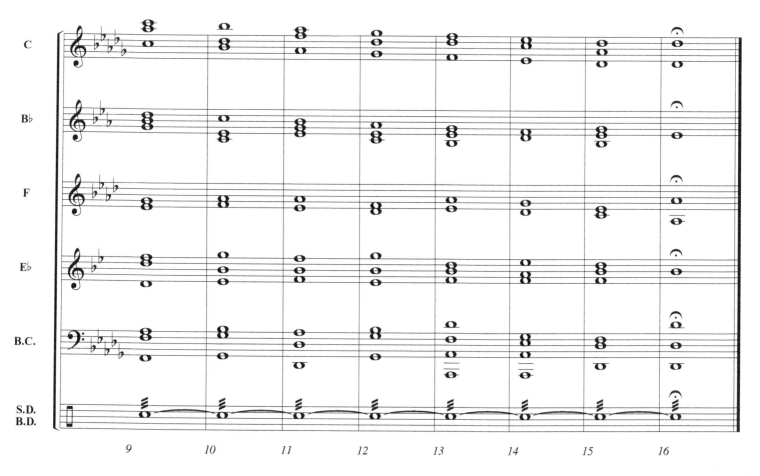

6 **Concert C Warm-up and Tuning Chorale**

Vary tempi and dynamic levels.

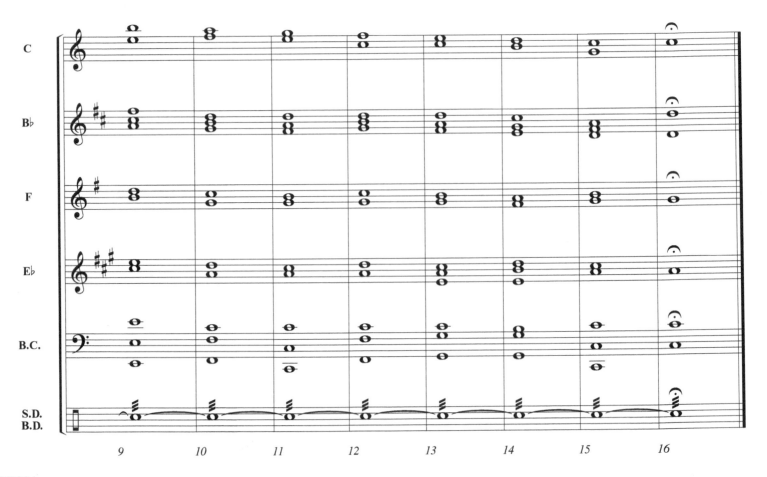

7 Concert G Warm-up and Tuning Chorale

Vary tempi and dynamic levels.

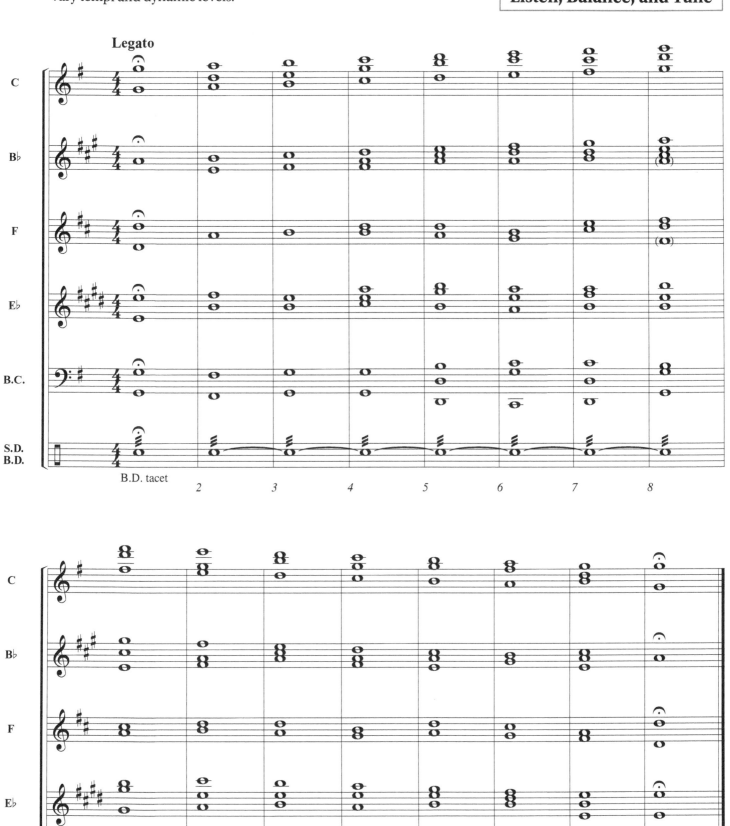

B.D. tacet

8 Concert D Warm-up and Tuning Chorale

Vary tempi and dynamic levels.

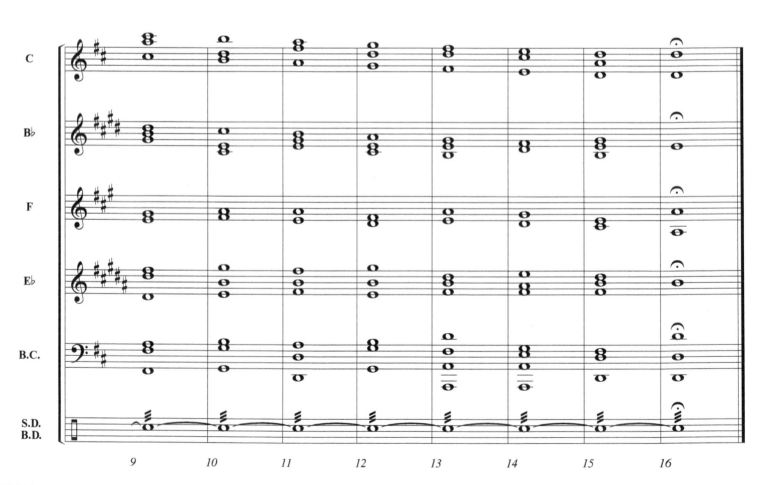

SECTION 4:
Intonation and Percussion Rudiments
Intonation and Tuning

The intonation test is designed to help you become aware of the pitch tendencies of your instrument. ***Intonation is an individual responsibility.*** When you are able to control pitch on your own instrument, the ensemble will begin to develop a better pitch center. You should try to go through this exercise several times each year to maximize results. The instructions for completing the test are listed here.

1. Work in pairs or have the section leader monitor the test for the section. Your director could also give the test by making individual appointments or focusing on a section at a time within each rehearsal.

2. Warm up and tune to a concert B♭ prior to starting the test. The monitoring student (or your director) should use an electronic tuner to record results on your test form.

3. Play the first note (indicated in the chart at the bottom of the test page) and hold a steady pitch for at least 8 counts (♩ = 88). During this time, the monitor should record the results of the pitch on the form. Use a plus sign (+) if the pitch is sharp and a minus sign (–) if the pitch is flat. The monitor should also record how sharp or flat each pitch is as indicated by the tuner, as in this example:

+10   –2   0   +7   –16   +15

4. Upon completion of the test, begin to make adjustments to any pitch that is equal to or greater than +/– 10.

5. Refer to the pitch tendency chart to make adjustments such as changes in embouchure, airstream and breath support, alternate fingers, and instrument modifications.

6. Your ultimate goal is for each pitch to come as close to 0 as possible. As your pitches move toward 0, the intonation of the ensemble will begin to show improvement.

Intonation Test*
Ranges may be adjusted to suit the needs of the student and at the director's discretion.

Range Indicator

Flute	33 – 59		**Trumpet**	23 – 49
Oboe	38 – 52		**Horn in F**	25 – 45
Bassoon	11 – 32		**Trombone**	11 – 33
Clarinet	20 – 52		**Baritone B.C.**	11 – 33
Alto Clarinet	20 – 45		**Baritone T.C.**	25 – 47
Bass Clarinet	19 – 45		**Tuba**	1 – 21
Contra Alto and Contra Bass Clarinet	20 – 45			
Alto Saxophone	30 – 52			
Tenor Saxophone	30 – 52			
Baritone Saxophone	30 – 49			

*Copy pages 74–75 as needed.

Intonation Test

Ranges may be adjusted to suit the needs of the student and at the director's discretion.

	A	A#	B	C	C#	D	D#	E	F	F#	G	G#
Test 1												
Test 2												
Test 3												
Test 4												
Test 5												
Test 6												
Average												
Range	1	2	3	4	5	6	7	8	9	10	11	12

	A	A#	B	C	C#	D	D#	E	F	F#	G	G#
Test 1												
Test 2												
Test 3												
Test 4												
Test 5												
Test 6												
Average												
Range	13	14	15	16	17	18	19	20	21	22	23	24

	A	A#	B	C	C#	D	D#	E	F	F#	G	G#
Test 1												
Test 2												
Test 3												
Test 4												
Test 5												
Test 6												
Average												
Range	25	26	27	28	29	30	31	32	33	34	35	36

Name: _____ Instrument: _____

BB204

Intonation Test

Ranges may be adjusted to suit the needs of the student and at the director's discretion.

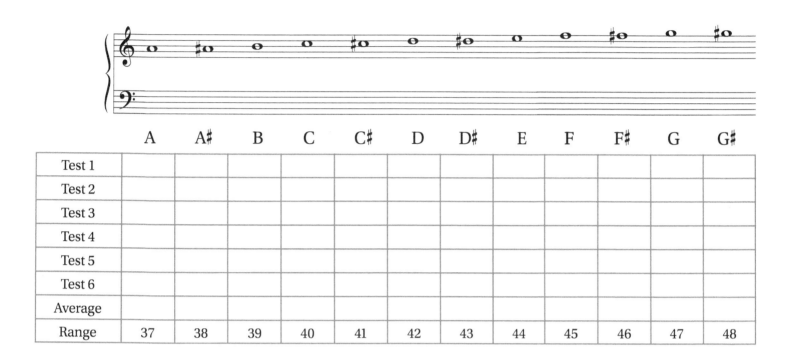

	A	A♯	B	C	C♯	D	D♯	E	F	F♯	G	G♯
Test 1												
Test 2												
Test 3												
Test 4												
Test 5												
Test 6												
Average												
Range	37	38	39	40	41	42	43	44	45	46	47	48

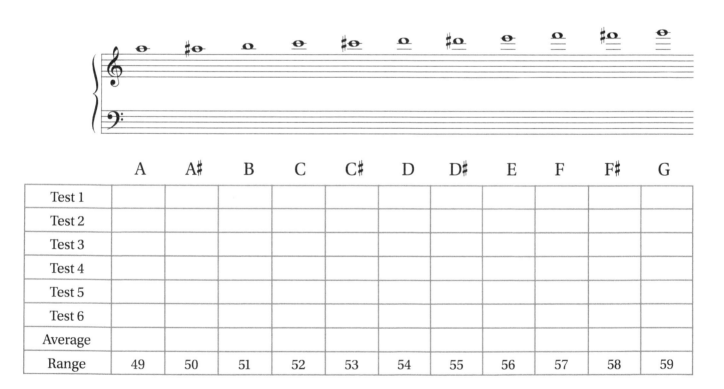

	A	A♯	B	C	C♯	D	D♯	E	F	F♯	G
Test 1											
Test 2												
Test 3												
Test 4												
Test 5												
Test 6												
Average												
Range	49	50	51	52	53	54	55	56	57	58	59

Name: _____   Instrument: _____

Pitch Tendencies and Adjustments

The following charts show pitch tendencies for notes that generally need adjustment on most instruments. Your intonation will begin to improve by becoming aware of the pitch tendencies of your instrument and implementing ways to alter those notes so they are closer to the pitch center. Your understanding of these concepts will be evident as you demonstrate better intonation skills.

Flute
MEMORIZE THIS INFORMATION

Sharp tendencies   Flat tendencies

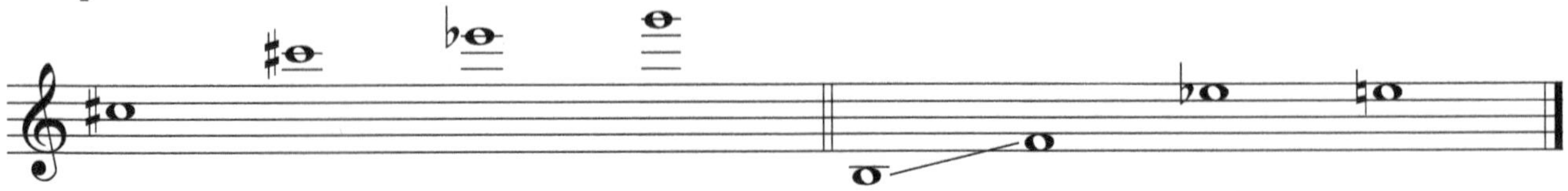

Sharp:

The flute will tend to play sharp when dynamics get louder. Notes in the upper range also have a tendency towards sharpness. At times, flute pitch may go sharp if too much air moves across the blow hole.

Pitch may be lowered through a variety of techniques including:

- rolling the flute in slightly
- slight shift of the head to help direct air downward
- slight shift of the embouchure to help direct air downward
- head joint adjustments, pull out
- alternate fingerings
- adding keys

Flat:

The flute will tend to play flat when dynamics get softer. Notes in the lower range also have a tendency towards flatness. Unsupported air and slower air speed will also cause the pitch to go flat. At times, flute pitch may go flat if too much of the blow hole is covered.

Pitch may be raised through a variety of techniques including:

- rolling the flute out slightly
- slight shift of the head to help direct air upward
- better air support
- slight shift of the embouchure to help direct air upward
- head joint adjustments, push in
- alternate fingerings

Oboe
MEMORIZE THIS INFORMATION

Sharp tendencies   Flat tendencies

Sharp:

The oboe will tend to play sharp in the upper range, especially above high Bb. Sharpness is also caused by pinching the reed or biting. At times, and depending on the quality of the reed, taking too much reed in the mouth may cause sharpness.

Pitch may be lowered through a variety of techniques including:

- directing the airstream downward
- slight relaxation of the embouchure to avoid pinching or biting
- adjusting the amount of reed in the mouth
- alternate fingerings

Flat:

The oboe will tend to play flat in the lower range. Unsupported air and slower air speed will also cause the pitch to go flat. Flatness is also caused by an embouchure that is unsupported or too relaxed. At times, and depending on the quality of the reed, taking too little reed in the mouth may cause flatness.

Pitch may be raised through a variety of techniques including:

- directing the airstream upward
- better air support
- slight increase in embouchure firmness
- adjusting the amount of reed in the mouth
- alternate fingerings

Bassoon
MEMORIZE THIS INFORMATION

Sharp:

The bassoon will tend to play sharp when dynamics get softer. The notes in the extreme lower range of the bassoon are usually very sharp. In the mid and upper ranges, G and G♯ will also be very sharp. Sharpness is also caused by pinching the reed or biting. The bassoon will tend to play sharp when dynamics get softer. The condition of the reed also contributes to pitch tendencies. A reed that is too hard will sometimes tend to play sharp. At times, and depending on the quality of the reed, taking too much reed in the mouth may cause sharpness.

Pitch may be lowered through a variety of techniques including:

- directing the airstream downward
- slight relaxation of the embouchure to avoid pinching
- adjusting the reed or selecting another
- adjusting the amount of reed in the mouth
- alternate fingerings
- change of bocal length

Flat:

The bassoon will tend to play flat when dynamics get louder. Flatness is sometimes prevalent at the upper end of the middle range. Flatness is also caused by unsupported air, slower air speed, and an embouchure that is unsupported or too relaxed. The condition of the reed also contributes to pitch tendencies. A reed that is too soft will sometimes tend to play flat. At times, and depending on the quality of the reed, taking too little reed in the mouth may cause flatness.

Pitch may be raised through a variety of techniques including:

- directing the airstream upward
- better air support
- slight increase in embouchure firmness
- adjusting the reed or selecting another
- adjusting the amount of reed in the mouth
- alternate fingerings
- change of bocal length

Clarinet (B♭, Alto, Bass, Contra Alto, and Contra Bass)
MEMORIZE THIS INFORMATION

Sharp tendencies   Flat tendencies

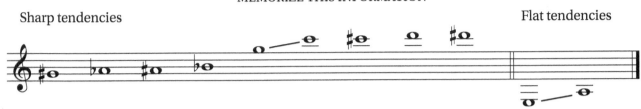

Sharp:

The throat tones on the clarinet tend to be sharp. Although not idiosyncratic, players should be aware that if they pinch in the upper range, this will err to the sharp side. Low clarinets will tend to be sharp in the upper range.

Pitch may be lowered through a variety of techniques including:

- directing the airstream downward
- slight relaxation of the embouchure to avoid pinching
- adjusting the amount of reed and mouthpiece in the mouth
- selecting a softer reed
- barrel adjustment
- alternate fingerings

Flat:

Low clarinets will tend to be flat in the lower range. Except when a student pinches, some notes in the upper range can go flat. Flatness is caused by unsupported air, slower air speed and an embouchure that is unsupported or too relaxed.

Pitch may be raised through a variety of techniques including:

- directing the airstream upward
- better air support
- slight increase in embouchure firmness
- adjusting the amount of reed and mouthpiece in the mouth
- selecting a harder reed
- barrel (neck) adjustment
- alternate fingerings

Saxophone (Alto, Tenor, and Baritone)
MEMORIZE THIS INFORMATION

Sharp tendencies   Flat tendencies

Sharp:

Notes in the upper range of the saxophone tend to be sharp. Third space C♯ and fourth line D are generally sharp. Sharpness is also caused by pinching the reed or biting. The condition of the reed also contributes to pitch tendencies. A reed that is too hard will sometimes tend to play sharp. At times, and depending on the quality of the reed, taking too much reed in the mouth may cause sharpness.

Pitch may be lowered through a variety of techniques including:

- directing the airstream downward
- slight relaxation of the embouchure to avoid pinching
- adjusting the amount of reed and mouthpiece in the mouth
- selecting a softer reed
- mouthpiece placement adjustment on the neck
- alternate fingerings

Flat:

Notes in the lower range of the saxophone tend to be flat. Flatness is sometimes caused by unsupported air, slower air speed and an embouchure that is unsupported or too relaxed. The condition of the reed also contributes to pitch tendencies. A reed that is too soft will sometimes tend to play flat. At times, and depending on the quality of the reed, taking too little reed in the mouth may cause flatness.

Pitch may be raised through a variety of techniques including:

- directing the airstream upward
- better air support
- slight increase in embouchure firmness
- adjusting the amount of reed and mouthpiece in the mouth
- selecting a harder reed
- mouthpiece placement adjustment on the neck
- alternate fingerings

Trumpet and Baritone T.C.
MEMORIZE THIS INFORMATION

Sharp tendencies   Flat tendencies

Sharp:

Pitch centering for many notes on brass instruments call for the performer to make subtle adjustments in breath support, air stream, and embouchure firmness. The notes listed above that are generally sharp need greater attention. In most cases, using trumpet valves in combination will raise the pitch center. As valves are used, the tubing length shortens. Therefore, in general, the more valves used in the combination, the sharper the pitch will tend to be.

Pitch may be lowered through a variety of techniques including:

- directing the airstream downward
- change in air speed
- slight relaxation of the embouchure
- adjust first and/or third valve slide
- alternate fingerings

Flat:

While flat tendencies for brass instruments are not as prevalent as sharp, some notes may border on flat. Generally this calls for the player to make natural adjustments in performance.

Pitch may be raised through a variety of techniques including:

- directing the airstream upward
- change in air speed and better air support
- slight increase in embouchure firmness
- alternate fingerings

Horn
MEMORIZE THIS INFORMATION

Sharp tendencies   Flat tendencies

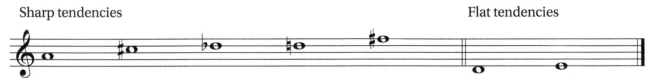

All brass players are encouraged to read the trumpet intonation sections on sharp and flat tendencies as the general concepts listed there apply to all valve brass instruments. Those playing double horn need to focus on intonation of both the F and B♭ slides. When all slides are completely inserted, many horns have been tooled to play a bit sharp. See trumpet intonation section on sharp and flat tendencies.

Pitch may be lowered through a variety of techniques including:

- directing the airstream downward
- change in air speed
- slight relaxation of the embouchure
- adjust tuning slide
- adjust valve slides
  (proportionate to length of the slide)
- alternate fingerings
- moving the hand slightly into the bell

Pitch may be raised through a variety of techniques including:

- directing the airstream upward
- change in air speed and better air support
- slight increase in embouchure firmness
- adjust tuning slide
- adjust valve slides
  (proportionate to length of the slide)
- alternate fingerings
- moving the hand slightly out of the bell

Trombone
MEMORIZE THIS INFORMATION

Sharp tendencies   Flat tendencies

Pitch centering on the trombone is fully reliant on the keen ear of the performer, as it works on a slide system rather than a system of valves. Each pitch is entirely alterable. Basic principles concerning breath support and embouchure listed in the trumpet section apply to trombone intonation. Additionally, there are certain notes on the trombone that naturally tend to be in need of alteration.

Pitch may be lowered through a variety of techniques including:

- directing the airstream downward
- change in air speed
- slight relaxation of the embouchure
- adjust tuning slide
- adjust slide position downward
- alternate slide position

Pitch may be raised through a variety of techniques including:

- directing the airstream upward
- change in air speed and better air support
- slight increase in embouchure firmness
- adjust tuning slide
- adjust slide position upward
- alternate slide position

Euphonium and Baritone B.C.

MEMORIZE THIS INFORMATION

Sharp tendencies   Flat tendencies

All brass players are encouraged to read the trumpet intonation sections on sharp and flat tendencies as the general concepts listed there apply to all valve brass instruments. The use of a fourth valve assists in correcting intonation in the lower range.

Pitch may be lowered through a variety of techniques including:

- directing the airstream downward
- change in air speed
- slight relaxation of the embouchure
- adjust tuning slide
- adjust valve slides (proportionate to length of the slide)
- alternate fingerings
- use of fourth valve

Pitch may be raised through a variety of techniques including:

- directing the airstream upward
- change in air speed and better air support
- slight increase in embouchure firmness
- adjust tuning slide
- adjust valve slides (proportionate to length of the slide)
- alternate fingerings
- use of fourth valve

Tuba

MEMORIZE THIS INFORMATION

Sharp tendencies   Flat tendencies

All brass players are encouraged to read the trumpet intonation section on sharp and flat tendencies as the general concepts listed there apply to all valve brass instruments.

The use of a fourth valve assists in correcting intonation in the lower range.

Pitch may be lowered through a variety of techniques including:

- directing the airstream downward
- change in air speed
- slight relaxation of the embouchure
- adjust tuning slide
- adjust valve slides (proportionate to length of the slide)
- alternate fingerings
- use of fourth valve

Pitch may be raised through a variety of techniques including:

- directing the airstream upward
- change in air speed and better air support
- slight increase in embouchure firmness
- adjust tuning slide
- adjust valve slides (proportionate to length of the slide)
- alternate fingerings
- use of fourth valve

Frequently Used Percussion Rudiments
MEMORIZE THIS INFORMATION

I. Roll Rudiments

1. Five Stroke Roll

R R L L

2. Seven Stroke Roll

R L R L
L R L R

3. Nine Stroke Roll

R R L L

4. Thirteen Stroke Roll

R R L L

5. Fifteen Stroke Roll

R L R L
L R L R

II. Diddle Rudiments

6. Single Paradiddle

R L R R L R L L

7. Double Paradiddle

R L R L R R L R L R L L

8. Single Paradiddle-Diddle

R L R R L L R L R R L L
L R L L R R L R L L R R

III. Flam Rudiments

9. Flam

L R R L

10. Flam Accent

L R L R R L R L

BB204

11. Flamacue

L R   L   R   L L R
R L   R   L   R R L

12. Flam Tap

L R   R R L   L L R   R R L   L

13. Flam Paradiddle

L R   L   R   R R L   R   L   L

14. Flam Paradiddle-Diddle

L R   L   R   R   L   L R L   R   L   L   R   R

IV. Drag Rudiments

15. Drag

L L R   R R L

16. Single Drag Tap

L L R   L R R L   R

17. Double Drag Tap

L L R L L R   L R R L R R L   R

18. Lesson 25

L L R   L   L   R L L R   L   R
R R L   R   L   R R L   R   L

19. Drag Paradiddle #1

R L L R   L   R R L   R R L   R   L   L

20. Drag Paradiddle #2

R L L R L L R   L   R   R   L R R L R R L   R   L   L

21. Single Ratamacue

L L R L R L R R L   L   R   L   R

22. Double Ratamacue

L L R L L R L R L R R L R R L   L   R   L   R

23. Triple Ratamacue

L L R L L R L L R L R L R R L R R L R R L   R   L   R

SECTION 5: Appendix
Rhythmic Counting
FOCUS, THINK, AND COUNT

These patterns may be used in a variety of ways.

1. Choose a single concert pitch for unison sound. Work on rhythm and balance at the same time by selecting different chord tones for each instrument family or group of the Balance Pyramid. Allowing each student to choose their own pitch might be a little dissonant but could be interesting and fun.
2. Select a measure and agree on how to count it. Your counting system should be consistent.
3. Perform the selected measure.
4. Perform rhythm patterns in larger phrases (5 measure, 10 measure, and so on).
5. This section may be used for rhythmic skills assessment. The patterns become progressively more complex. Let students perform to see how far they can go before making a mistake.

Festival Preparation
NOTES TO THE DIRECTOR

1. Spend quality time in the selection of literature. Identify styles that are appropriate for your venue. A good rule of thumb is to choose a couple of pieces of contrasting styles so that you showcase the capabilities of your ensemble. Carefully check the festival requirements. Some may call for specific works, others might require you to choose from certain titles, while others might let you select your own program without any parameters other than time.

2. After narrowing down the styles, select several titles within the style that will be appropriate for your ensemble situation. Take time in initial score study so that you become aware of the musical challenges students will face. While you might be able to select after having studied the scores, some tunes will require the students sight-reading the piece for you to decide whether or not it is appropriate and viable.

3. Once you have made at least two and up to four selections, it could be in the best interest of the students to program these for a concert that occurs just prior to the festival. This will give you and the students an opportunity to perform the works. The few days between the concert and festival performances can serve to solidify performance practices.

4. Your initial score study should be followed with more intense score study. A performance analysis is a good way to address the musical elements, the probable needs of the students, and the development of teaching and rehearsal strategies. Don't shy away from using a professional recording as you study. Some criticize this practice, but we have found it helpful in the complete understanding of the work. In particular, focus on things *musical*. A big difference between good band performances and great band performances is the evidence of expression and musicianship. In your study and subsequent rehearsal, concentrate on expressive items such as dynamic movement, articulation contrast, style, entrances and releases in phrasing, tension and release, and the cultivation of inner supporting lines.

5. Analysis should lead to rehearsal techniques that will assist the students in rendering the intended interpretation. Mark your score to remind you of conducting techniques and the decisions you made during score analysis. List anticipated potential problems for each instrument. These should be addressed in your rehearsal plans.

6. The students will need to understand that they are responsible for all musical elements. Remember: you can't get to the *music* if the basic elements are not there. Student practice should involve work in technique, rhythmic accuracy, tone quality, and the like.

7. Remember to use as many outside resources as will enhance learning. The use of professional recordings of the works you are rehearsing is a great way of reinforcing musical ideas. Provide recordings for students and a method by which they can access them.

8. Engage in self-evaluation and criticism. Record your rehearsals on a regular basis. Review the recording to help you develop the plan for the next rehearsal. On occasion, play a recording for the students and let them discuss what needs to be the next focus. You will also want to engage in videotaping so that you can review your conducting effectiveness and the students' response to your gestures.

9. Just as you engage in self-evaluation and criticism, the process should also involve an element of on-going assessment of student progress and achievement. The main components of correct notes, rhythms, dynamics, and articulations are critical and primary for the further development of musicality. Periodic assessment of student achievement in these areas will ensure success.

10. Discuss the festival process with your students ahead of time. In some instances, they will have the opportunity to work with an adjudicator following their performance. Instruct them in listening to the suggestions of the clinician and being open to trying things in a new or different way. Remind students of the reason for performing at a festival. You are there to help them improve as musicians. The focus should be on the learning and the performance. If you are wrapped up in scores and trophies, you and your students will lose sight of the bigger and better picture.

11. In the festival, use the warm-up room to get your students engaged mentally. Warm-up routines help them to concentrate on very specific musical ideas. They can be mind-clearing activities. Take advantage of this time and avoid demonstrating performance anxiety, as this will certainly affect the performance.

12. Live performances always require musicians to remain engaged and alert. The festival performance is no different. They should listen and watch for musical elements that might change, even slightly, in the performance. This is particularly true if your ensemble is performing in that space for the very first time. Adjustments will be necessary and they would be well advised to stay alert.

Note to the Students

Be responsible for knowing your part to the best of your ability.

Listen and decide how you should adjust for balance, blend, and intonation.

Always use the best possible technique.

Make beautiful music.

Enjoy and learn from this experience.

Glossary of Terms

Tempo (Markings associated with the speed of music)

Accelerando – (accel.) Gradually getting faster little by little

Adagietto – A little faster than *Adagio*

Adagio – A slow speed (♩ = 66–76)

Allegretto – A little slower than *Allegro*

Allegro – A fast speed (♩ = -160)

Andante – A moderate walking speed (♩ = 76–108)

Andantino – A little faster than *Andante*

Larghetto – A slow speed (♩ = 60–66)

Largo – A slow speed in a dignified manner (♩ = 40–60)

Lento – A very slow tempo

Moderato – At a medium speed (♩ = 108–120)

Ritardando – (rit.) Gradually getting slower

Style (A manner of playing)

Espressivo – Play with expression

Legato – (–) Play in a smooth and connected manner

Marcato – Play in a short and stressed manner

Sostenuto – Play in a sustaining manner

Staccato – (·) Play in a short, light, and detached manner.

Dynamics (Degrees of softness and loudness)

Pianissimo – (***pp***) Very soft

Piano – (***p***) Soft

Mezzo Piano – (***mp***) Moderately soft

Mezzo Forte – (***mf***) Moderately loud

Forte – (***f***) Loud

Fortissimo – (***ff***) Very loud

Crescendo – (*cresc.* or ◁———) Gradually getting louder

Decrescendo – (*decresc.* or ———▷) Gradually getting softer

Other Musical Elements

Accent – (>)Indicating that a note should be played with stress or emphasis

Chorale – A hymn-like composition that should be played in a *legato* style

Chromatic Scale – A scale that proceeds up or down in half-steps

Divisi – (div.) An indication for the players to divide into two or more groups

Ensemble – Refers to a group of two or more musicians playing together

Etude – A musical study that usually focuses on a technical aspect

Fermata – (⌢)An indication that a note or rest should be held longer

Repeat Sign – (‖: :‖) An indication to go back to the beginning of the piece or to another repeat sign

Tie – (⌣)A curved line connecting two or more notes of the same pitch so that they are played as one combined note